D1129859

OCT 0 4 2013

Published in 2013 by The Rosen Publishing Group, Inc.
29 East 21st Street, New York, NY 10010

Photo Credits: **KEY** r=right; tl=top left; tc=top center; tr=top right; cl=center left; c=center; cr=center right; bl=bottom left; bc=bottom center; br=bottom right; bg=background

CBT = Corbis; GI = Getty Images; iS = istockphoto.com; N = NASA; PIC = The Picture Desk; SH = Shutterstock; TF = Topfoto; TPL = photolibrary.com; wiki = Wikipedia

front cover bl SH; **back cover** bc iS; cl SH **1**c TF; **2-3**bg TPL; **6**bc, bl, cr SH; **7**br, tl CBT; tr iS; **8-9**c GI; **10-11**c TF; **11**br SH; **12**cl CBT; **12-13**c TPL; **13**br TPL; **15**cr N; **16**cl TPL; **16-17**bc TPL; **17**cl TF; cr TPL; **18**bc, tl TPL; **19**bg CBT; **20**c CBT; tl GI; **21**bg GI; **22**bl GI; br CBT; tr TF; **23**bc GI; tl PIC; tr TF; **24**bl GI; cl TF; **24-25**bg GI; **26**bl GI; br SH; cl iS; **27**br, tc iS; c SH; **28**c CBT; bc TF; cl wiki; cr TPL; **29**bl, tc N; br CBT; cl TF; tr GI; **30**c, cr, bg SH; **31**br TF; **32**cr SH

All illustrations copyright Weldon Owen Pty Ltd.

Weldon Owen Pty Ltd
Managing Director: Kay Scarlett
Creative Director: Sue Burk
Publisher: Helen Bateman
Senior Vice President, International Sales: Stuart Laurence
Vice President Sales North America: Ellen Towell
Administration Manager, International Sales: Kristine Ravn

Library of Congress Cataloging-in-Publication Data

Brasch, Nicolas.
  Robots of the future / by Nicolas Brasch. — 1st ed.
      p. cm. — (Discovery education: technology)
  Includes index.
  ISBN 978-1-4488-7885-7 (library binding) — ISBN 978-1-4488-7967-0 (pbk.)
  ISBN 978-1-4488-7973-1 (6-pack)
  1. Robotics—Juvenile literature. 2. Robots—Juvenile literature. 3. Robotics—Technological innovations—Juvenile literature. I. Title.
  TJ211.2.B726 2013
  629.8'92—dc23
                         2011051536

Manufactured in the United States of America

CPSIA Compliance Information: Batch #SW12PK: For Further Information contact Rosen Publishing, New York, New York at 1-800-237-9932

ROBOTS OF THE FUTURE

NICOLAS BRASCH

PowerKiDS press.

New York

Contents

Types of Robots

There are many different types of robots. Some are built to make work easier or safer for humans. Others are built for amusement. Humans always control robots and determine what and how they operate. Some robots are controlled by human-designed computer programs, while others are maneuvered by a remote control device.

Humanoid robot
A humanoid is a robot that looks like a human. Some have only the basic physical features. Others have some of the human senses, such as touch, sight, and hearing.

Robotic arm
Robotic arms are robots that have several movable joints, similar to a human arm. They carry out tasks faster, and with more accuracy and reliability, than a human could. Robotic arms are most common in factories.

Robot on wheels
Some robots do tasks that are extremely dangerous or difficult for humans. A robot-miner is able to detect the presence of bombs or land mines—a job that saves putting human lives at risk.

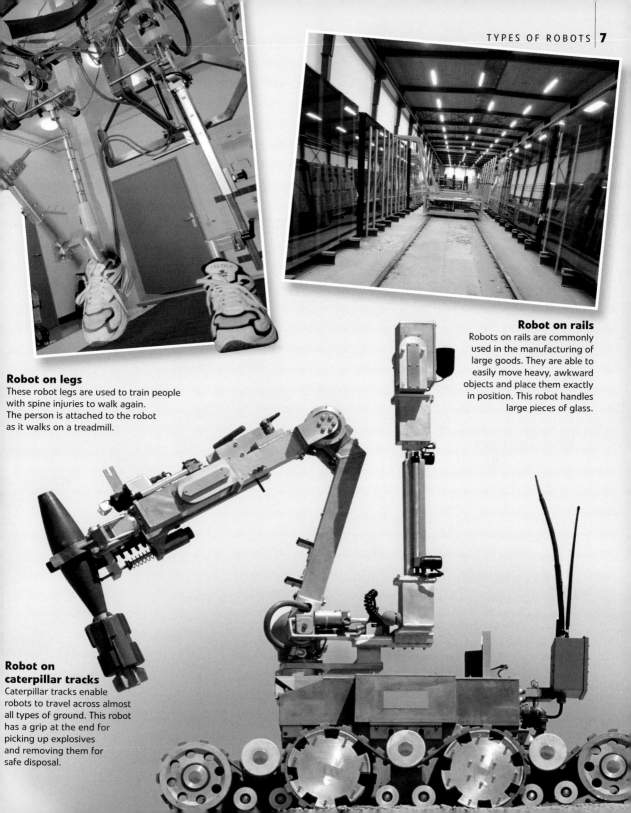

Robot on rails

Robots on rails are commonly used in the manufacturing of large goods. They are able to easily move heavy, awkward objects and place them exactly in position. This robot handles large pieces of glass.

Robot on legs

These robot legs are used to train people with spine injuries to walk again. The person is attached to the robot as it walks on a treadmill.

Robot on caterpillar tracks

Caterpillar tracks enable robots to travel across almost all types of ground. This robot has a grip at the end for picking up explosives and removing them for safe disposal.

Robot Parts

While there are many different types of robots, most have a body with movable, individual parts. These parts often copy human movements. For example, a robotic arm has movable joints that work in a similar way to the human elbow or wrist. Some humanoid robots walk on legs and can pick up objects with their hands.

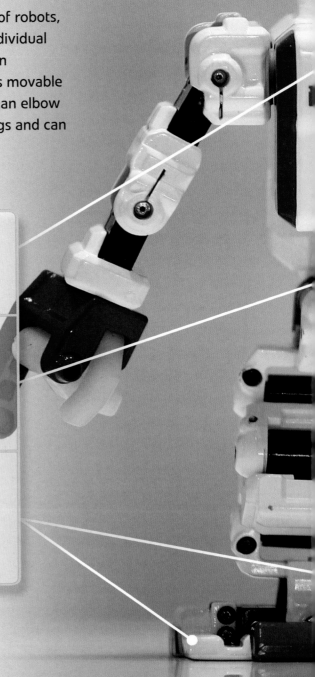

Light sensors

A light sensor works by detecting visible or infrared light bounced off objects around the robot. This function enables robots to navigate toward or away from other objects.

Sound sensors

A sound sensor detects sound waves bouncing off an object. This provides more information about the robot's environment and allows it to know how far it is from certain objects. Robots can also be built with a speech recognition device, which enables them to react to voice instructions.

Pressure sensors

Some robots have pressure sensors, similar to the human sense of touch. These sensors usually have two purposes. They let the robot know when it has bumped into something and should change course, and they allow robots with arms and hands to grab and pick up objects correctly.

Internal power source

Robots must have a power source to be able to operate. Some robots use batteries. Others have solar cells, which convert light into energy. Mechanical robots, however, are wound up.

Internal controller

Every robot has a controller, which is basically a computer operating system. It contains all the information that allows the robot to carry out its tasks and commands. The controller is the robot's equivalent to the human brain.

REMOTE CONTROL

Robots that are sent to other planets, such as the Mars Sojourner, have controllers inside them but can also be operated remotely from Earth. They have cameras that send images back to Earth and based on these images, the operator can determine where the robot should move and what tasks it should perform.

Robots in Industry

R obots have been used in industry for more than 50 years. Some of these robots are able to perform faster or more precisely than humans, while others can move heavy objects more easily. Robots can do the same task over and over again without getting bored. Another advantage in using robots is that they require far fewer breaks. While they have to be repaired and maintained, they do not need to sleep, take bathroom breaks, or go home to look after their family.

The car industry

At an automotive factory in Germany, more than 450 industrial robots work in the body shop. Some robots weld parts of the car bodies together, while others guide small pieces into place. Some laser-bond windows into position, and others fill each vehicle with exactly the right amount of the correct grade of fuel.

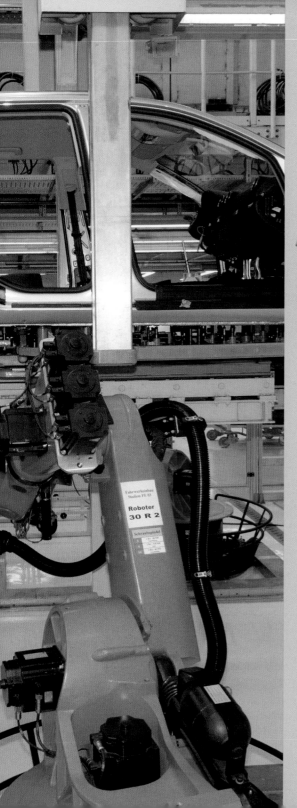

Six-axis robot

An axis is a point around which something rotates. Many robots in industry have six axes. Each axis enables the robot to move in a particular way.

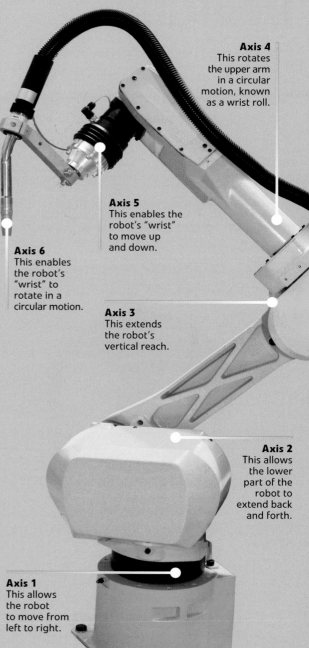

Axis 4
This rotates the upper arm in a circular motion, known as a wrist roll.

Axis 5
This enables the robot's "wrist" to move up and down.

Axis 6
This enables the robot's "wrist" to rotate in a circular motion.

Axis 3
This extends the robot's vertical reach.

Axis 2
This allows the lower part of the robot to extend back and forth.

Axis 1
This allows the robot to move from left to right.

Robots in Medicine

One of the best examples of how robots can be used to help humans is the use of robots in medicine. Sometimes robotic surgery involves robots playing only a minor role. Doctors can use robotic instruments to do time-consuming or difficult jobs more quickly and efficiently than they could using just conventional medical instruments. However, in some types of surgery—such as certain cardiac operations—robots can play a major role.

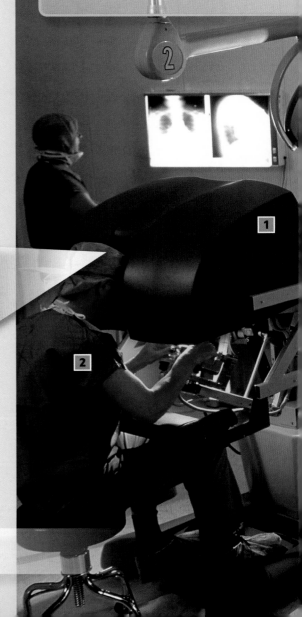

Operation in progress

A cardiac operation is carried out by a robot known as the da Vinci System. A surgeon manually controls the robotic arms. There are other robotic systems that respond to verbal commands. In the future, medical procedures using robots will become more common.

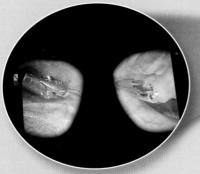

A surgeon's view
Cameras attached to the robot provide the surgeon with a close-up view of the procedure taking place.

Surgery can now take place with the surgeon in one location and the patient in another.

1 Close-up view
The surgeon's console sits several feet from the operating table. Cameras attached to the robotic arms provide the doctor with a close-up, 3-D, high-definition view of the procedure.

2 Using joysticks
Despite not standing over the operating table, the surgeon is still in control throughout. The surgeon moves the robotic arms using joysticks similar to those used on video game consoles.

3 Multifunctional
The robotic arms perform several functions including cutting, sewing, removing organs, and relaying images to the surgeon and other medical staff.

4 Displaying images
Images of the operation are relayed to a screen so that medical staff assisting the surgeon can see what is happening.

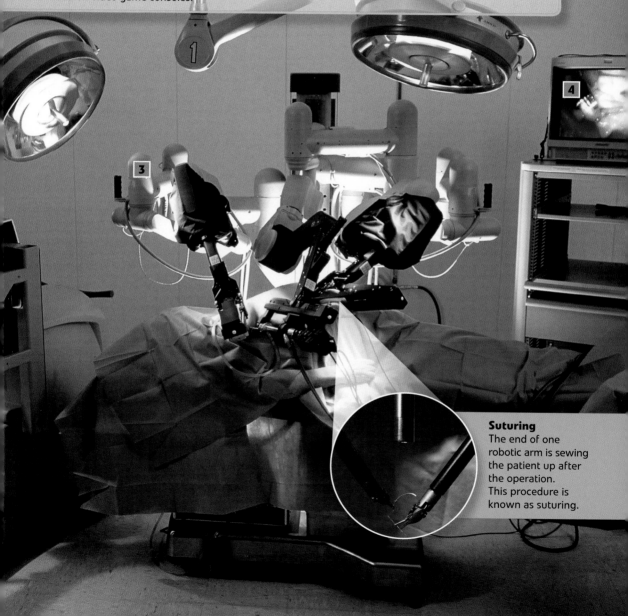

Suturing
The end of one robotic arm is sewing the patient up after the operation. This procedure is known as suturing.

Robots in Space

Robots have often seemed like something out of science fiction, so it should be no surprise that they are used in space. Robots are perfect for this because they can operate for a long time in an environment that humans could only visit for a short time. Robots have been sent into space since the 1960s. Some of them have simply flown past other planets and sent back photos and other data; others have landed on planets, carried out extensive surveys, and collected samples to be sent to Earth for further examination.

Spectrometer
This is for conducting detailed examinations of rock and mineral samples.

Rover robots

NASA, the US space agency, sent two robots to Mars in 2003. Known as the Mars Exploration Rovers, they landed in January 2004 and since then have been closely examining the "red planet." Their main aim is to find evidence of past water activity on Mars. The rovers have many special instruments.

CENTAUR

NASA has developed a robot astronaut known as Centaur. It is a half-humanoid, half-vehicle robot that was used in the Arizona desert as part of NASA's testing of the next generation of space equipment. Another NASA robot, the SCOUT rover, is able to transport both astronauts and equipment, follow verbal commands and hand signals, take direction by wireless remote control, and relay communication and images.

Centaur, with SCOUT behind

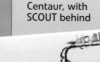

Camera
This is for taking images of the surface.

Magnet
This is for collecting magnetic dust particles.

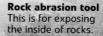

Rock abrasion tool
This is for exposing the inside of rocks.

That's Amazing!

NASA has developed a robonaut, which is a robot built to look and operate like a human astronaut. Robonauts can survive in space longer than people and carry out dangerous tasks.

LEGO robot

The toy brand LEGO has been around since 1932. In recent years, it has released robot models. They might be toys, but they have many features of more complicated robots, such as sensors, controllers, and power sources. This robot can follow commands and play volleyball against another LEGO robot.

RCX 1.0

Robot World Cup

This event is held every year. Teams construct and program robots that compete against other teams in games of soccer. The ultimate aim is to use these soccer games to develop advanced robotics and artificial intelligence technology.

Jupp

Playing with Robots

Toy robots have become increasingly popular, especially in Japan. Some are controlled by a remote control device; others respond to voices and other sound signals, such as hand claps. Although they are toys, the research and technology that is required to create them is helping to advance the field of robotics.

Robot dog
This robot dog has been designed to act and respond in the same way as a real dog. It barks, walks, begs, and obeys certain voice commands. It can also cock its leg in the same way that male dogs do.

Toy baby robots
RealCare Baby II is a rechargeable robot that acts and reacts like a very young baby. It must be fed, burped, rocked, and diapered around the clock. It responds only to its primary caregiver, who must wear wireless identification when caring for the baby.

Where Humans Fear to Tread

Robots are the ideal solution for locations that are too dangerous or remote for humans. Apart from space, these include underwater, in deserts, inside volcanoes, and in war zones. Even if humans are able to enter such places, they cannot function for very long without a rest. Robots do not need food or water, can be fitted with long-lasting batteries or solar panels, and can be made to withstand extreme heat and cold.

Dante volcano robot
This volcano robot is able to enter volcanoes, even when they are erupting. It can take gas and other samples and relay the information to scientists in a safe location. This Dante robot explores the crater of Mount Spurr, in Alaska.

Underwater exploration
The Remora 2000 submarine and the Super Achilles ROV often operate together, searching the ocean bed for shipwrecks and other relics. The submarine holds two observers. The Super Achilles is a robot that performs several functions, including photographing objects, taking samples, and recovering submerged items.

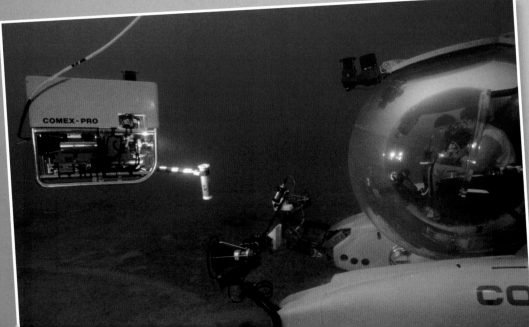

Bomb disposal
A remote–controlled robot examines a box during a security demonstration. Because of the threat of terrorist activity around the world, bomb disposal robots need to be able to carry out many different types of operations. The most modern versions are able to open overhead lockers in planes and buses, and search underground.

Around the Home

Many robotics experts believe that in the future, robots will become a normal feature of most homes. The main reason for this is that people want their lives made as easy as possible for them. They want someone, or something, else to do the hard, boring, dirty tasks that they hate. And robots are perfect for such roles.

Washing dishes
Few people enjoy washing dishes but this robot does not complain. While this scene may not be common in homes for some time, Panasonic and the University of Tokyo have developed a robotic arm that rinses plates and then loads them into a dishwasher.

Leading the way
The Japanese company Toyota may be best known for producing cars but it is also researching robot technology. It aims to produce robots that support people's everyday lives. In 2007, Toyota's then-president, Katsuaki Watanabe, unveiled some of their robot creations.

Mobility robot
This can follow its owner, carry heavy goods, negotiate steps, and travel up to 3.7 miles per hour (6 km/h).

Violin-playing robot
In the future, humanlike robots may be built to entertain, as well as help with vital tasks.

Robina
This robot guide can be programmed to give instructions and directions to human tourists.

Walking the dog

Creating a robot that walks a dog may seem like fun, but it has a serious side. Such a robot would be good for elderly people who want a dog as a companion but cannot walk the dog. The robot could also be used to guide the elderly on walks.

Robots in Fiction

References to robot-like figures in fiction date back to ancient Greece. Today, robots are a popular feature of many books, magazines, movies, television shows, and even songs. Some fictional robots have made an enormous impression on our minds. The word "robot" was first used in a work of fiction. It appeared in a play by the Czech writer Karel Čapek in 1920. The word comes from the Czech word *robota*, which means "hard work."

The Daleks

Daleks are robot-like figures from the television series *Doctor Who*. While their metallic appearance, mechanical movements, and automated responses are similar to other fictional robots, they sometimes express emotions, which is unrobot-like.

Astro Boy

Astro Boy first appeared in a Japanese magazine in 1952 and has since been the star of a television series and a movie. Astro Boy is a crime-fighting humanoid robot, with super strength and flying rocket boots.

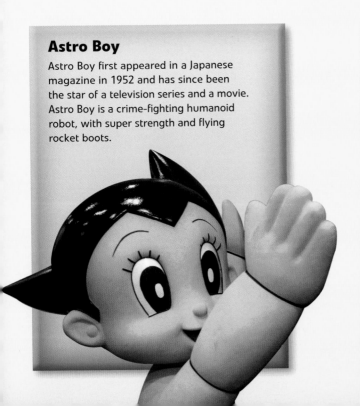

R2-D2

R2-D2 is a character from the *Star Wars* movies. He stands just 3 feet 2 inches (0.96 m) tall and chirps and whistles to communicate with others. He is good at understanding complex computer systems, which helps him to rescue others from danger.

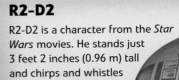

The Terminator

Terminators are humanoid robots from the series of *Terminator* movies. The first terminator, who was played by Arnold Schwarzenegger, was a trained assassin built by the military.

Robots, the movie

Robots is a movie in which all the characters are robots. Many of the robots have human traits, particularly the main characters, Rodney Copperbottom and Fender.

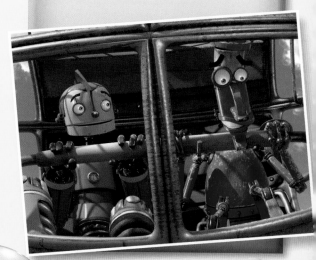

Bender

Bender is a character from the television series *Futurama*. His humanlike characteristics emphasize the worst aspects of human behavior.

Artificial Intelligence

Artificial intelligence—or AI for short—is a branch of computer science and engineering. It aims to create programs that enable machines to function and learn in intelligent ways. Such machines should not be confused with computers, which only process information according to directions given to them by humans. Artificial intelligence machines must be able to think and learn for themselves.

ASIMO
ASIMO is a humanoid robot that can recognize human faces and gestures, and respond in an appropriate, personal manner.

Facial recognition

Facial recognition technology is an example of a type of artificial intelligence known as learning systems. These systems allow a computer to recognize patterns and make decisions based on these patterns. Facial recognition systems have to process many different factors and match them to information within their databases.

DEEP BLUE

Deep Blue was a computer programmed to play chess against the world's best players. World chess champion Garry Kasparov played six matches against Deep Blue in 1997. The computer won three, lost two, and drew one.

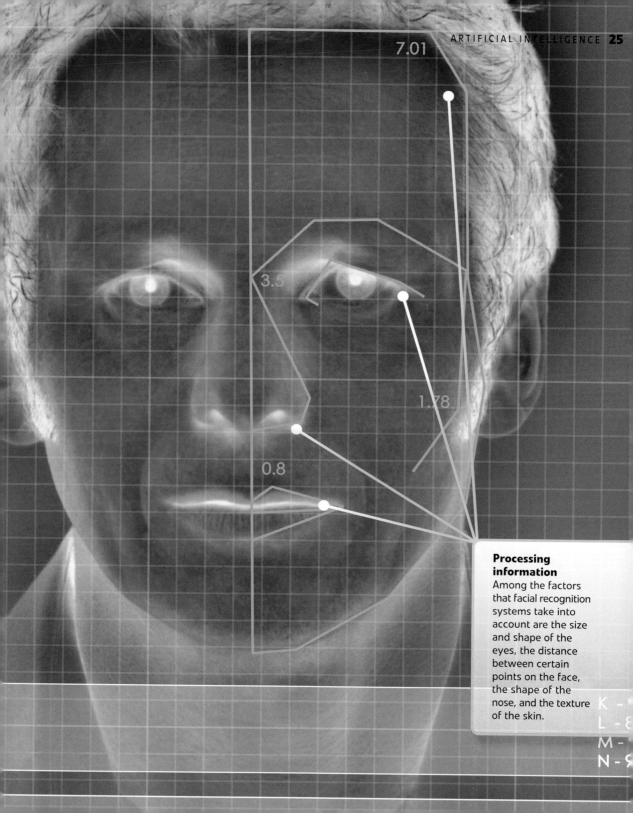

7.01

3.5

1.78

0.8

Processing information
Among the factors that facial recognition systems take into account are the size and shape of the eyes, the distance between certain points on the face, the shape of the nose, and the texture of the skin.

K - *
L - 8
M -
N - 9

?... You Decide

Robots and the technology that helps create them have had a major impact on the way many humans live their lives. However, few things in the world are 100 percent positive. The question is: will robotic research and technology do more good for humans than bad? You decide!

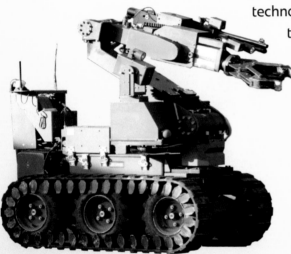

Pros of robots

Many of the jobs robots do are tasks that humans are either unable or unwilling to do. Some robots explore areas of Earth and beyond, helping to make humans more knowledgeable about their surroundings. And some robots, such as those used in medical operations, can even save lives.

On the front line
Some robots are able to identify and then defuse bombs or land mines.

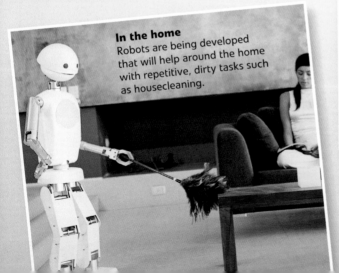

In the home
Robots are being developed that will help around the home with repetitive, dirty tasks such as housecleaning.

Industrial robots
An industrial robot is able to carry heavy loads and perform precise movements that are beyond the ability of humans.

Cons of robots

Science fiction is full of tales of evil robots or robots that have gone crazy and started acting independently of the humans who created them. But there are other reasons to fear robot technology, such as their potential to make humans unnecessary in many areas of life, including the workforce.

Out of work

Robots can perform without a rest—except when being repaired—and do not complain about working conditions. Some businesses would be better off with robots than with human employees. The result could be long lines of unemployed people.

UNEMPLOYMENT LINE

Out of control

Some people fear that robot technology could become so advanced that robots would have the ability to think, act, and react for themselves. If this is the case, what is to stop them from attacking humans and taking over the world?

Development Time Line

Robots are thought of as a modern invention but the idea of creating machines that look and operate like humans has been around for hundreds of years. Indeed, there are references to robot-like creatures being used by the gods in ancient Greek literature.

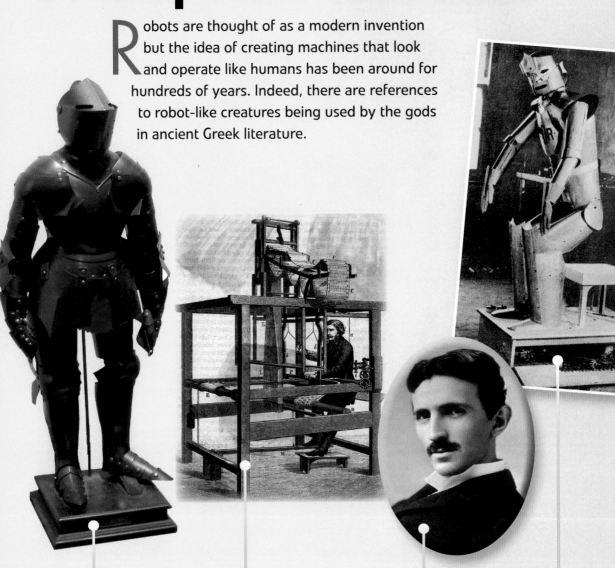

1495
Leonardo da Vinci creates a mechanical knight to show that human movement can be imitated. More recently, NASA creates anthrobots, with humanlike features.

1801
Joseph Jacquard invents a textile machine called a programmable loom. It is operated by punch cards. This machine does the work of several humans.

1890s
Nikola Tesla designs the first remote control vehicles. Today, many robots are controlled by remote devices.

1920
The first reference to the word "robot" appears in a play by Karel Čapek. The play is called *Rossum's Universal Robots*.

1941
Science fiction writer
Isaac Asimov first uses
the word "robotics" to
describe the technology
of robots, and predicts
a robot industry.

1976
Robot arms are
used on the
Viking 1 and 2
space probes
that are sent
to explore Mars.

1997
NASA's Pathfinder
lands on Mars. In
one month, it sends
back more than
16,000 images of
the Martian surface.

2000
Humanoid robots
that replicate human
movement are
unveiled by Japanese
companies, such as
Honda and Sony.

2004
The toy humanoid
Robosapien
is created by
Canadian physicist
and robotics expert
Dr. Mark W. Tilden.

Design Your Own Robot

Building a robot might be expensive, but there is nothing to stop you from designing one.

Before you start designing your robot, you need to think about the following questions:

1 What is the main purpose of your robot—for example, to amuse, clean, or perform difficult tasks?

2 How will it move—for example, on legs, wheels, rails, or caterpillar tracks?

3 How will it be powered—for example, by battery, solar cells, or a wind-up mechanism?

4 What features will it have—for example, light sensors, sound sensors, pressure sensors, cameras?

Once you have answered these questions, you can design and sketch your own robot. Then get your friends to do the same, and compare the results.

What you need:

☑ Paper

☑ Pencil

☑ Eraser

Glossary

automated
(AH-tuh-mayt-ed) Operated
without direct human assistance.

cons (KAHNZ)
Disadvantages.

database (DAY-tuh-bays) A
storage system for information.

disposal (dih-SPOH-zul)
The action of getting rid
of something.

humanoid robot
(HYOO-muh-noyd ROH-bot) A
robot that looks like a human.

internal (in-TUR-nel) Inside.

laser–bond (LAY-zer-bahnd)
To join two things together using
a laser.

loom (LOOM) A machine used
to make textiles.

manufacturing
(man-yuh-FAK-cher-ing) The
making of something.

mobility (moh-BIH-lih-tee)
The ability to move.

navigate (NA-vuh-gayt) To
work out a route and follow it.

pros (PROWZ) Advantages.

robotics (roh-BAH-tiks)
The science of creating and
studying robots.

solar cell (SOH-ler SEL) A
device that captures energy
from the Sun and converts it
into electricity.

spectrometer
(spek-TRAH-mih-ter) An
instrument that inspects tiny
pieces of rocks and minerals.

weld (WELD) To join metals by
applying heat.

Index

A
artificial intelligence 16, 24–25
ASIMO 24, 29
Asimov, Isaac 29
Astro Boy 22

B
Bender 23

C
Čapek, Karel 22, 28
Centaur 15
controller 9, 16

D
da Vinci, Leonardo 28
da Vinci System 12, 13
Daleks 22
Dante 18
Deep Blue 24
Doctor Who 22

F
facial recognition 24, 25

H
humanoid 6, 8, 15, 22, 23, 24, 29

I
industrial robot 10, 11, 26

J
Jacquard, Joseph 28

K
Kasparov, Garry 24

L
learning systems 24
LEGO 16
light sensor 8, 30

M
Mars Exploration rovers 14, 15
mobility robot 20

N
NASA 15, 28, 29

P
Pathfinder 29
pressure sensor 8, 30

R
R2-D2 22

RealCare Baby II 17
Remora 2000 18
Robina 20
robonaut 15
Robosapien 29
Robot World Cup 16, 17
robotic arm 6, 8, 12–13, 20, 29
robotic surgery 12, 13
Robots (movie) 23

S
SCOUT rover 15
six-axis robot 11
solar cell 9, 30
sound sensor 8, 30
space robots 9, 14, 15
spectrometer 14
speech recognition 8
Star Wars 22
Super Achilles 18

T
Terminator 23
Tesla, Nikola 28

Websites

Due to the changing nature of Internet links, PowerKids Press has developed an online list of websites related to the subject of this book. This site is updated regularly. Please use this link to access the list: www.powerkidslinks.com/disc/robot/